HOLY OIL AND ELBOW GREASE

LOUISE KIRK

Holy Oil
and
Elbow Grease

Practical and Spiritual Tips for
Running a Busy Home

ST PAULS

ST PAULS Publishing
187 Battersea Bridge Road, London SW11 3AS, UK
www.stpauls.ie

Copyright © ST PAULS 2002

ISBN 085439 654 3

Set by TuKan DTP, Fareham, UK
Printed by Interprint Ltd., Marsa, Malta

ST PAULS is an activity of the priests and brothers
of the Society of St Paul who proclaim the Gospel
through the media of social communication

Contents

Introduction

I made a wondrous discovery some months ago: pair dirty socks by turning over the tops and they have some hope of entering the same machine-load. Better still, place them in string bags and they emerge from the machine still united and ready to dry in sorted rows. I told a friend of how I was saving some ten minutes a wash and she said, 'I have long been doing that.' 'Why didn't you tell me?' I exclaimed, though I can see that socks are a subject which might not come up in conversation.

Earlier I had discovered another, more far-reaching truth, which is that prayer does not need to be confined to the moments when one is on one's knees, or even to those extra thoughts which may wing their way heavenwards during the day. Every action, especially our work, can be offered to God as prayer if it is done with love and to the best of our ability. As this novel approach to faith sank in, the whole panorama of my day as a busy mother and housewife changed. No longer was it irksome to peel a dozen potatoes: each one could be offered for a person or intention, and the home become a mission land whose influence could extend far beyond four walls.

This appealing truth has implications. When there are many demands upon one's time, how does one carry out each task well? Not by attaining perfection: that much is clear in any active household, especially one in which children romp and friends come to call. What is important is to strive to do one's best and to improve day by day within the many limits of time and circumstance. This means being organised and introducing into the home some of the disciplines found in a modern office, such as goals, guiding principles and action plans.

As I struggled to think of ways to make my own life more efficient, it occurred to me that there must be a pool of helpful solutions worked out by friends and acquaintances which could be shared. So it was that the idea of this booklet came to be: a collection of practical household tips spiced with some spiritual quotations from the Bible and from great men and women who have inspired me. Since much of my own thought has been shaped by St Josemaría Escrivá I have also included a dedication to him, with an explanation as to why he is a modern-day saint for the housewife.

I am most grateful to the many people who have given me tips for this booklet. The 'I's do not of course belong to one person, but I have retained some to keep the personal tone in which they were given.

Housekeeping in a modern context

The technological revolution of the home is a subject rarely focused upon in its own right. At the beginning of the last century the number of people employed in domestic service in England reached into the millions, but it has never been fashionable to point this out, and there was certainly no union to represent the sector or make protest at its demise. A new machine here, cling film and ready-cut salads there, and over the years the whole panorama of housekeeping has been simplified beyond recognition. It has needed to be, because in addition to her having little paid help in the house, the demands on the housewife have changed. Many combine keeping house with full- or part-time jobs, while the children who used to help their mothers are kept in education. It is true that men contribute more to household tasks than of old, but statistics stubbornly show that, despite popular rhetoric, the bulk of the work and certainly overall responsibility is still carried out by women. Leisure is not a word familiar even to those younger people who are based full-time in the home. Most do so because they have children, and these they take to classes and on expeditions while they themselves are often active in the community, for instance in their child's school.

Housework of old was real physical work in a way that mercifully it is no longer. Mixing a cake by hand, laying and cleaning out fires, washing both laundry and dishes by hand, was hard slow work. However, there is a cost to the modern revolution which is easily overlooked: because she is working quickly, the housewife no longer has time to muse and think things through slowly, but is making constant small decisions at the rate of someone in an office, while usually doing several other things at the same time. The work has changed in emphasis to become more mental than physical, though she will still be on her feet all day, wielding machines and dusters when not running to the car.

The housewife is a manager in a job for which the training is ever diminishing. It is just assumed that a young woman will know how to run a house even when she may have spent her earliest years at a nursery and subsequent ones in full-time academic education. When both parents work there is even less opportunity to develop her domestic skills. This exclusive bias in modern education is despite the fact that most women will need to run a home for a large part of their lives.

Saint Josemaría Escrivá

St Josemaría Escrivá is best known as the divinely inspired founder of Opus Dei, a Personal Prelature of the Catholic Church, whose members aspire to live and pass on a message of universal application: that sainthood is a realistic goal for everyone and that most people achieve sanctity through their ordinary life and especially through their work. He was an organised man himself and had the sensitivity to his surroundings of the architect he might have been. The home to him was not just a place where people eat and sleep but where families are nurtured and draw the strength they need to develop their human potential. At a time when servants were still the norm in the middle- and upper-class households of his native Spain, he foresaw that the pressure upon women to develop careers, while having much good in it, would tend to diminish the esteem in which homemaking skills are held. This in turn would eat away at the structure of happy family life and at the gentleness of society as a whole. Later in his life he pointed to the materialism of a society which categorises women not by the nature of their work but by whether or not it is paid. Language itself is powerful, and he would have loved to have removed the terms 'working' and 'non-working' mothers. Homemaking he declared to be not only work but a profession, and one of the greatest, at that.

It is no accident that, in the face of contrary trends, homemaking was to become a special characteristic of Opus Dei, in the houses of its married members and also in all the Centres of the Work. St Josemaría was no stranger to housework himself. When he first set up a students' residence, he had not the money for the expected domestic help and so, unseen and despite the huge number of his other commitments, he would clean and make the beds. Later his mother and sister took over housekeeping and they became examples to those women of Opus Dei who dedicate their professional lives to the hospitality of the Centres. Some run catering courses to spread their expertise more widely.

The standards that St Josemaría set are high. Little things matter, he repeatedly said, because it is in doing the little things well that the big things follow. Each act can be offered as a service to others and also as a prayer to God. But what counts most is not the excellence of the result but the struggle and the love which has been put into it. That is what will make us saints.

St Josemaría was not, however, someone who believed that women should be kept at home. He had huge regard for feminine skills, and was all for their being used in every profession that was appropriate to their dignity and to their family life. The heroism of a saint is not only spiritual but also human, taking on a lot and doing everything well! To achieve the role in society which he encouraged means running the home efficiently, and I thought that in his now perfect heavenly home it would tickle him to be given this booklet as a birthday present for his centenary on 9 January 2002, now crowned by his canonisation on 6 October.

General principles

Professional work – and the work of the housewife is one of the greatest of professions – is a witness to the worth of the creature. It provides a chance to develop one's own personality; it creates a bond of union with others; it constitutes a fund of resources; it is a way of helping in the improvement of the society we live in, and of promoting the progress of the whole human race …

For a Christian, these grand views become even deeper and wider. For work, which Christ took up as something both redeemed and redeeming, becomes a means, a way of holiness, a specific task which sanctifies and can be sanctified.

(St Josemaría Escrivá, *The Forge*)

'Oh, you've got five children, so I suppose you don't work?' A close friend expostulating on the stupidity of some people's comments remarked that a reason to love St Josemaría is that he recognised work when he saw it. He did more than that. He saw in ordinary situations a grandeur that passes most of us by. One video catches him beaming from ear to ear as he talks about the value of housework, which might seem

exaggerated if one did not realise that he was praising the profession of the two women he loved most, his mother on earth and Mary, his mother in heaven.

The purpose of a well-run house is to make life easier and happier for those who live in it and to make it an attractive port of call for those who visit. The running of the house should never take priority over the people it is there to serve.

Running a house well is never finished. We all of us run out of time, money and energy, probably in that order, before our aspirations are anywhere near to being fulfilled. Living cheerfully with these shortcomings and one's own incompetence is sometimes difficult but never impossible.

The mistress of the house is a manager, as the name implies, even when she has only herself to manage. Learn to delegate as much as possible, especially to children but also to husbands. It is often harder to do this than to do the job in hand, but don't give up! After all, it is charitable to train others to look after themselves.

One of the main handicaps to the efficient running of a house is having too much inside it. Ideally, everything in the house should both serve a purpose and have a place, *one* place and only one.

It helps to focus on what is worth acquiring if you remember that for everything you do have you don't have something else: another dress, less space in the cupboard; a new machine now, less happy anticipation – as well as money.

Most of the struggle we have with surplus things is sentimental: when you buy things for yourself, you can choose them, but when other people give them to you it can be very difficult to give them away. Heroic effort is sometimes needed to recognise that dear Aunt Joan will never know that you haven't kept her pincushion. Some things we should keep, but beware too many.

It is easy to get rid of something when you know someone who will use it; it is hard to do so when you don't know how to dispose of it usefully. I long for the system common in some Continental countries whereby large items can be left outside the door on particular days for collection by whomsoever. Perhaps we should suggest it here. For smaller items it helps to collect them in one place so that they are ready for the next jumble sale, charity collection or car boot sale.

Distinguish between the 'flowers' and 'diamonds'. Some things, such as sticker books, have glorious but brief lives: it is best to recognise that the pictures will never be coloured in and get rid of the book instead of cluttering up a drawer. Think too about what you are passing on to others. Sometimes it is most charitable in our affluent society to throw something away.

Sentiment is particularly dangerous when it comes to paper. Keeping a magazine because a splendid organisation took trouble to prepare it is not good enough if you are not also going to read it. If in doubt, throw away. Dusty piles do not assuage the conscience, and by getting rid of the clutter you will actually have access to the material you will use.

When a piece of equipment will make a difference to you, don't feel guilty about buying it. Everyone recognises that an office needs to be updated periodically, and the house is no different. One might even encourage machines to break down every fifteen years or so. Technology does move on!

Domestic organisation

'From that hour onward, the disciple took her into his home' (Jn 19:27). Can the same thing be said of us? Do we also take Mary into our home? We should welcome her with full title into the home of our life, our faith, our affections, and our commitments. We should acknowledge the motherly role that is proper to her – as dispenser of guidance, advice, and exhortation, or simply as a silent presence, which at times is enough to infuse strength and courage into us.

(John Paul II, *A Year with Mary*)

Images of Mary are dotted around our house. I address them in different ways as I go about my business; my most direct conversations tend to be with Our Lady Over the Sink. To her I often have recourse when I need some quick help, and to her I complain on the many occasions when things go wrong. Her assistance in domestic organisation is practical, lighthearted and very real.

Making constant decisions is stressful and also wastes time. The purpose of keeping an orderly house is so that you don't have to think so much and so that others know the system too. Thinking through a plan of action at the beginning of the day also simplifies decision-making (see Time Management, below). Routines are the other great standby.

To keep the house in order, go around it once a week, collect all the 'bits and bobs' left here and there and put them exactly where they should be. If you are lucky enough to have a cleaner, it is a good discipline to do the tidying before she arrives, and also to empty the vacuum cleaner and write her a list of tasks.

Everything should have a place, but sometimes the same thing is regularly needed in two places, e.g. shoe polish. Double up, then, and have it in both.

Every household has paper and needs a filing system, be it in a cabinet or in plastic trays. These are cheap and can be labelled with Dymo tape.

Mending is another nightmare which weighs upon the stressed housewife. Have an attractive shopping bag ready to hand complete with all you need for the next few tasks and seize it en route to the doctor, dentist, or child's lesson. I get in at least half an hour a week.

Packing is equally traumatic when done frequently with a sizeable family. Computers make packing lists much more realistic. A first list can be quickly altered for different circumstances until you have a whole sheaf of lists ready to the button. Take your list with you and amend it when you reach your destination so that it will be more accurate next time. Lists can also be handed to children so that they do the job themselves.

If you travel frequently, have a separate ready-packed wash-bag, etc., in a drawer. It may be useful to extend this to a permanent bottle-bag with basic medicaments for the family.

Sympathetic lighting helps every task, especially when jobs are dull. Modern spotlights and other systems don't have to be expensive and make one feel more efficient.

Save yourself journeys by leaving ready things to take up and downstairs, but don't then ignore the hopeful piles because you are in a hurry: you will be in a hurry next time, too.

Small children do not need separate bedrooms. When children share there are fewer rooms to clean and heat and the nuisance value of their keeping each other awake is amply repaid by the special friendships that form in the dark. Used to being together at home, they are also more adaptable when camping in someone else's house.

We quickly get used to ugliness, which is a pity. Try to act quickly when something breaks or is out of order, and hide the baskets of ironing.

Time management

When you bring order into your life your time will multiply and, as a result, you will be able to give greater glory to God, by working more in his service.

(St Josemaría Escrivá, *The Way*)

Time is like money: for most of us, most of it is pre-committed so that our flexibility is small. The art is to be organised and at the same time relaxed at the many interruptions which always happen in a house. Heroism is to smile at them.

Start the day at a fixed time. Try to wake up a quarter of an hour before the children. Those fifteen minutes will help you to start the day calmly and get plenty done.

If possible, breakfast should have been cleared before leaving for school (training of husband and children may be necessary here). The coming home after dropping off the children is thus less depressing and the day starts more promptly.

Air the rooms and beds thoroughly during breakfast. Thirty minutes in the morning refreshes the room while saving on heating. Children should also be taught to make their own beds as soon as possible, but do be patient and make sure that they can physically do what you are asking of them. Even pulling up a duvet can be more difficult than it looks when a child is small and the bed is in a corner.

Either first thing or after breakfast prepare a rough timetable for the day. Include slots for prayer, reading, and relaxation too. It is a good idea to set aside half an hour a day for paperwork.

It can help to have ongoing lists for such things as telephoning, letters, special household tasks and the garden, into which you can jot when something occurs to you. Going through these lists jogs the memory when preparing the time-table, and makes sure that things don't get forgotten even when they are yet undone.

Timetables are usually too ambitious, particularly when you first start. Why not actually time various standard tasks so that you have a more realistic idea of how to piece them together and what small job you can add in when you have a few spare minutes?

Think creatively about the tasks which take you longest. If you cannot cut down the time commitment, you may be able to fit in something else as well.

Your programme once made is bound to be interrupted, if not overturned. Continuing to strive for efficiency while always being smilingly adaptable is the struggle of a lifetime.

Storage ideas

It is the working man himself who most benefits from work thus understood. Not because he gets his wages for his work, but because the work, that is bound inseparably with his person, shapes and develops his mind, will, feelings, various moral virtues and characteristics, his physical and spiritual skills. This is what St Paul means when he reminds us: The first share in the harvest goes to the labourer who has toiled for it.

(Stefan, Cardinal Wyszynski, *Work*)

Cardinal Wyszynski's little book **Work** *made a profound impact upon me when I first read it. It is full of the most wonderful insights into the value of human endeavour which has become fundamental to my own way of thinking. When work is tough, and for me there is nothing tougher than having to tidy up a house, I often remind myself that it is 'the working man himself who most benefits from work thus understood'.*

Every single thing in the house has to have one – and only one – place. It takes a little bit of organising at first but it saves so much time looking for missing items and it means easy and fast tidying up. Even a playroom can be tidy in less than three minutes given a row of shelves and many labelled plastic storage boxes.

Sort children's writing implements into separately marked sweet jars or upright picnic boxes. These can be conveniently stored on a shelf – with only one jar being used at a time!

Question regularly whether everything is in the most convenient place. (For example, do I use that particular machine so often that I should keep it permanently on the kitchen worktop? If not, should it be in the cupboard close to hand, or in the garage at one remove?)

Hang your bicycles in the garage with hooks set in the ceiling.

Keep many big plastic boxes (if possible with mouse- and dust-proof lids) clearly labelled according to ages. Neatly pile into these the children's clothes which are in abeyance and it will become a joy to fish for them again when they are needed.

Wind elastic bands around the ends of your coat hangers to prevent clothes from slipping off.

Store children's clothes where they are most convenient for you rather than for them. If you are able to centralise some it will save extra trips when putting away.

If you have big teenagers who leave all their mess everywhere, keep one box per child in a handy place and fill it with whatever you find in the house that belongs to them. Periodically empty the boxes on to the appropriate beds and leave the owners to sort out the mess. And remember to return the boxes to their own places.

Cleaning

There is no work in the performance of which man can be shut up wholly in himself. In every type of human work there is a bond with some other work that has already been done – a connecting link in the work itself: work done before this binds together the past and the future. Whatever we take up in the course of our work, we see, enclosed in its completed form, the incarnated work of the past. The work which we add to the work already done, will itself be taken up by our successors, who will develop it, improve it, perhaps, and bring it one stage further. In the same way, a man at work now is linked with the man who worked before him and with the man who will come after him. There exists a sort of special 'communion of saints' in work and through work.

(Stefan, Cardinal Wyszynski, *Work*)

Another aspect of Cardinal Wyszynski's book which has had an influence upon me is the idea that all work brings one into close communion with other people even when it is performed in isolation, as is so much of housework. There is no reason to feel alone.

When preparing food, I often cast a thought upon the people who first produced it as well as upon those who shortly will eat it. However, it is in cleaning that my imagination runs freely. Furniture reminds me of the people who gave it to me, of those who made it, and those who have cleaned it in the past. I prefer not to think of those who will soon dirty it again.

Have a set day for cleaning the house – and keep to it! For example: every Thursday, prepare for the weekend by a thorough clean, so leaving Friday free for shopping/cooking; every Monday, repair the damage of the weekend by a quick hoover and tidy. Carpets collect dust, so by hoovering twice a week you can the more easily dust only once.

Carry with you on your rounds a box with all the different polishes/cloths you will need ready assembled. A deep ice-cream box is the right size.

When cleaning curtain tracks, use a furniture polish – it will also make the hooks run freely.

A quick way to clean venetian blinds: wear an old pair of gloves, dip fingers in warm soapy water, and then draw each slat between the fingers.

Ordinary soap and water on a Scotchbrite green scouring cloth quickly removes daily greasemarks from baths and basins without having to leave out the detergents children so love to play with.

Use handwash in place of soap in all washbasins and they won't become so dirty in the first place! Those with moisturisers keep hands better, too.

Bubblebath has a similar effect in the bath – though may be less good for the skin.

The new limescale-removing lavatory cleaners are much better than traditional ones for removing stains. The tablets are particularly easy to use.

Bicarbonate of soda added to the cleaning water will freshen up the inside of the fridge and freezer.

Get rid of stale smells in a room with a quick spray of soda water.

Don't throw away old towels – keep one to hand for mopping up spills, and another for washing the car.

Use a hairdryer to dust dried flower arrangements.

Revive your piano keys with a soft cloth dampened with milk.

Shoe polish that is hard or lumpy can be softened with a few drops of paraffin, turpentine or olive oil.

A few drops of washing-up liquid in a little warm water make spectacles sparkle.

Treat yourself to a new vacuum cleaner if you haven't had one recently. The new bagless variety is excellent.

Stain removal

> O wash me more and more from my guilt
> and cleanse me from my sin.
> My offences truly I know them;
> my sin is always before me.
> Against you, you alone, have I sinned;
> what is evil in your sight I have done.
>
> (Psalm 51:2-4)

Souls, tablecloths, carpets: a single stain on what is otherwise clean ruins the whole. I try to remember at some point during the day to offer up a few acts in reparation for my own sins and for those of others, particularly the souls in purgatory (whose help I am in turn not shy to ask!). Rubbing at a stubborn stain while reciting King David's memorable words is curiously satisfying.

White rings on polished furniture are greatly reduced by rubbing olive oil into them with your fingers. Leave it to soak in, and polish off with a good beeswax polish. The sooner you spot the problem the better.

If very hot water and a nail brush refuse to

move children's glue, varnish remover (and patience) will do the trick.

To remove candle wax from tablecloths, press a warm iron on to some kitchen paper over the stain and the wax should all be absorbed.

Blood on clothes should be kept damp. As soon as possible, wet the stained area thoroughly, lay it flat and pour on a thick coating of salt. This should soak up all the blood.

Neat washing-up liquid rubbed into stains down shirt fronts will usually remove them after rinsing.

Drip stains on carpets and upholstery can often be rubbed away with WetOnes. These wipes, sold alongside nappies, are worth having for a great many uses, not least in the car.

Laundry

You have let a soul slip through your fingers. The howl of sharpened famine for that loss re-echoes at this moment through all the levels of the Kingdom of Noise down to the very Throne itself. It makes me mad to think of it … By Hell, it is misery enough to see them in their mortal days taking off dirtied and uncomfortable clothes and splashing in hot water and giving little grunts of pleasure – stretching their eased limbs. What, then, of this final stripping, this complete cleansing?

(C.S. Lewis, *The Screwtape Letters*)

An old Italian fable describes the servant who complains at having to clean his master's boots.

'What is the point of cleaning them when tomorrow they will be dirty?'

'Just so,' says his master.

When the servant comes for his dinner, he finds the table bare.

'What is the point of feeding you when by tomorrow you will be hungry?'

Laundry is a very repetitive business, and I hope it causes as much joy in heaven as grief in hell.

Socks clipped together by turning over their tops have a hope of entering the same machine-load together. Put them into string in-wash bags and they will emerge still united, ready to be dried in neat paired rows. Train your family to do the pairing, and also to undo buttons and empty pockets.

In-wash bags are also invaluable for delicates, including tights. They can be used too to sort the clothes of different family members when they become responsible for their own washing.

If you have the room, sort the dirty laundry into categorised baskets by the machine. It is then obvious which load is needed next and filling the machine is quick. Four baskets is about right.

A laundry basket per person/room helps to sort the loads and trains lazy children into using one. If you don't want to buy baskets, an old pillowcase suspended on a wire hanger behind the door does the trick and needs no sewing.

Have a set day when everyone changes (for example) sheets and pyjamas.

White shirts will be whiter if first soaked in Biotex.

Watch fabric conditioners on towels. The coated fibres lose absorbency so that they feel soft but dry less well.

If zips don't run easily, rub a lead pencil along them and you'll find they fly.

Ironing

You must be careful: don't let your professional success or failure – which will certainly come – make you forget, even for a moment, what the true aim of your work is: the glory of God!

(St Josemaría Escrivá, *The Forge*)

Do people hate ironing because it is time-consuming or because it shows up those who aren't good at it? I once gave a less competent au pair what I thought were foolproof instructions and returned to find a large hole in a blouse. A radio programme I happened upon changed ironing for me.

The secret of good ironing is to take even more care over the cloth than over the movements of the iron. Having made sure that you have a good ironing surface, be it table or board, and that the iron is at the correct temperature, some golden rules are:

- Always iron damp and never be without a water spray, even if you have a steam iron.
- Iron in the right order. Small areas of cloth

recrease less easily than the large ones with which you should finish. A shirt, for instance, should always be begun with the collar, cuffs and sleeves, followed by the back and ending with the two (more exposed) fronts.

- Keep moving the material so that the piece about to be ironed really is flat. You will probably spend as much time moving and folding the cloth as actually ironing it.

To prevent clothes becoming shiny, buy a Bettaware Ironing Cloth. It looks like very stiff lace.

You won't need to iron heavier weight skirts if, as soon as you undress, you hang them in a convenient place and spray them with water. The creases will fall out overnight.

Hide the ironing basket and its contents! If you can't tackle it immediately, cover it with plastic or a damp cloth to keep the contents moist and dispose of it where it will not depress you and the other members of the house. Should you be in the happy position of designing a new kitchen/utility room, why not include a special cupboard with rails on which to hang the damp and ironed shirts, with shelves below for baskets? I have often thought one out in my head!

Much of the ironing is taken out of sheets and tablecloths if you pull and shake them straight (preferably with a helper) and fold them carefully while still a little damp. They will keep ready for ironing for some time spread on a table or over a rail.

When the sole-plate of the iron becomes scorched, try rubbing the warm iron (unplugged) over a candle stub rolled in a couple of layers of cotton or linen over an old towel. Then rub the iron into the towel itself to remove remaining wax before continuing to iron. If something is very stuck, try placing a damp clean Brillo pad on an old towel, then rub the warm iron over the Brillo pad until the sole-plate is smooth. Clean the sole-plate, including the edges, with a damp piece of towel before continuing to iron.

If you have an Aga or similar cooker, use its chrome lids to press the household linen and many clothes. Aga ironing is an art in its own right. Some starting points are:

- Fold a small pile of clothes carefully on the lids when damp. Watch the enamel surrounds of the cooker, which are hotter and can scorch.

- Turn over the clothes periodically until each is pressed. The drying can be finished on the airer.

- Use the boiling plate lid with extreme caution as it can scorch.

- Don't put dark clothes on light as they can run.

- Keep ready a water spray to dampen dry areas.

Cooking

Saint Martha was holy, though we are not told that she was contemplative; and what more do you want, than to become such as was this blessed woman, who deserved so often to entertain Christ, our Lord, and to give Him sustenance, to serve Him, and to eat at His table? … Remember, it is necessary that someone should cook the food, and think yourselves happy in serving with Martha; recollect that true humility largely consists in being very ready to be satisfied with what the Lord wishes to make of us, and always to consider ourselves unworthy to be called His servants.

(St Teresa of Avila, *The Way of Perfection*)

Cooking is the most creative part of housework. One has the impression that Martha enjoyed it and was very good at it, sparing herself no pains in producing the best for her Lord and his entourage. What a sympathetic figure she is as she protests to Jesus that she has been left alone by her sister to cope with what must have been a large crowd of visitors. Had she spoken earlier to Mary and been given a brush-off? Or had Mary promised to come and been unable to drag herself away? One can see the gentle smile on

Jesus' face as he calls Martha lovingly by her name and chides her, not for being busy, but for fretting and so forgetting to listen for him in her work. It is noticeable that it is she rather than her sister Mary who is celebrated in the liturgical year.

The food processor is one of the most useful kitchen machines. Always buy the biggest available regardless of the size of your household as you can then make and freeze double quantities.

Save washing the processor, which is tedious by hand and space-consuming by machine, by tackling tasks in the right order, e.g. pastry first (which leaves it all but clean), followed by slicing apple, followed by making a cake. If you are slicing salads, start with the palest ingredients first. When you have the processor out, make and freeze some bags of breadcrumbs, too.

It is cheaper and often better to make your own grated cheese than to buy it. Use the processor to grate a large pack and freeze it in small bags.

Don't wait until you need to bake to make your pastry. Mix the flour and fat and keep them in the refrigerator in an airtight container until needed. All you have to do later is add the water. If you rub a little oil on to your hands, it prevents the pastry from sticking to them.

Grated chocolate is a surprisingly useful larder ingredient. When you next need some, grate a whole bar on to greaseproof paper and funnel the extra into a screwtop jar. It keeps well, and tastes so much better than bought substitutes.

The meat for a traditional beef stew doesn't have to be sealed. Roll it in seasoned flour with herbs to taste, and cover with onions well flavoured by long slow cooking in butter and oil and a little sugar. Add carrots, stock/wine, other flavourings, and cook the lot slowly in the normal way. Nobody will know that you saved yourself all that spitting fat.

Aged citrus fruit need not be wasted: pop some inside a chicken and it will greatly improve the flavour. Windfall apples can likewise be used.

Stock is improved by first baking the bones for twenty minutes in a moderate oven. Add an onion, topped and tailed but unpeeled, some vegetables if liked, a stock cube or two and the water, and boil in the usual way. Slices of lemon will freshen aged bones.

Ice cubes added to the hot stock will encourage the fat to congeal so that it can be skimmed without cooling.

Freeze stocks, soups, etc., in a standard box lined with a freezer bag. When the liquid is frozen, remove the box and the resulting block will stack neatly with others of similar shape.

Leftover mincemeat makes a delicious bread and butter pudding.

Wilting lettuce can be revived in twenty minutes by soaking it in cold water with a good dash of vinegar.

If sugar has gone hard, empty it into a bowl, cover with a damp cloth and leave in a warm place for an hour or two.

The ripening of an avocado pear is speeded up if you store it in a paper bag with a banana. Equally, bananas will ripen other fruit in a bowl more quickly; if inconvenient, store them separately.

This morning after completing my spiritual exercises, I began at once to crochet. I sensed a stillness in my heart; I sensed that Jesus was resting in it. That deep and sweet consciousness of God's presence prompted me to say to the Lord, 'O most Holy Trinity dwelling in my heart, I beg You: grant the grace of conversion to as many souls as the number of stitches that I will make today with the crochet hook.' Then I heard these words in my soul: *My daughter, too great are your demands.* 'Jesus, You know that for You it is easier to grant much rather than a little.' *That is so, it is less difficult for me to grant a soul much rather than a little, but every conversion of a sinful soul demands sacrifice.* 'Well, Jesus, I offer you this whole-hearted work of mine; this offering does not seem to me to be too small for such a large number of souls; You know, Jesus, that for thirty years You were saving souls by just this kind of work. And since holy obedience forbids me to perform great penances and mortifications, therefore I ask You, Lord: accept these mere nothings stamped with the seal of obedience as great things.' Then I heard a voice in my soul: *My dear daughter, I comply with your request.*

(St Faustina Kowalska, *Divine Mercy in My Soul*)

Cooking is made up of many small tasks which can be offered for different souls. Each bean to be sliced, each carrot to be pared, can be offered for another friend or intention. I can never peel a potato without thinking of the priest who first impressed this upon me.

Peel potatoes and other vegetables over newspaper. All the mess can then be quickly rolled up and binned.

Halve onions and lay them flat before attempting to dice them. It makes the job so much easier.

Oranges are quicker to peel if soaked in boiling water for ten minutes and then in cold.

Cauliflower becomes lovely and white if milk is added to the cooking water.

Use scissors in place of a knife wherever possible, e.g. for cutting up pizzas, herbs, children's spaghetti.

The easiest way to separate an egg is to break it into a saucer, put an upturned glass over the yolk and pour off the white.

Don't throw away an old hot-water bottle without first cutting from it some large discs. These are wonderful for opening stubborn jars and bottles. Use one at the top and one at the bottom of the jar if it is really difficult.

The most difficult task for me was draining the potatoes, and sometimes I spilt half of them with the water. When I told this to Mother Directress, she said that with time I would get used to it and gain the necessary skill. Yet the test was not getting any easier, as I was growing weaker every day. So

I would move away when it was time to drain the potatoes. The sisters noticed that I avoided this task and were very much surprised. They did not know that I could not help in spite of all my willingness to do this and not spare myself. At noon, during the examination of conscience, I complained to God about my weakness. Then I heard the following words in my soul, *From today on you will do this easily; I shall strengthen you.* That evening, when the time came to drain off the water from the potatoes, I hurried to be the first to do it, trusting in the Lord's words. I took up the pot with ease and poured off the water perfectly. But when I took off the cover to let the potatoes steam off, I saw there in the pot, in the place of the potatoes, whole bunches of red roses, beautiful beyond description. I had never seen such roses before. Greatly astonished and unable to understand the meaning of this, I heard a voice within me saying: 'I change such hard work of yours into bouquets of most beautiful flowers, and their perfume rises up to My throne.'

(St Faustina Kowalska, *Divine Mercy in My Soul*)

Would that St Faustina had had my new saucepan from Aldi whose lid can be held on from the handles, but then she would not have witnessed the lovely miracle of the roses which must be an encouragement for many other hardworking cooks. Our Lord's tender solicitude is so touching: he allows St Faustina to suffer and die young from the most painful of diseases because suffering united to his cross has a redemptive value beyond our understanding, but he also helps her with a saucepan to show her how much he cares. I have often found that when big prayers remain unanswered small favours come to raise my spirits.

When draining potatoes, rice or pasta, put cold water into the sink to reduce the risk of the steam burning your hands.

Teflon non-stick cooking liner, available from supermarkets, is an excellent invention. The lining washes (even in the dishwasher, though it can be simpler to soak and wash it by hand). Cut shapes once to suit your favourite baking tins and they can be reused for evermore.

Pop whole bananas into a dish in the oven at a medium temperature for 20–30 minutes until the skins are black. Open carefully with scissors and fork. They will look limp, but taste delicious and have a surprising amount of juice.

Breadmakers make wonderful bread. They have come right down in price and are very easy to use and clean. You can also use them to make jam and fruity cakes, the latter being mixed and baked automatically in the one container – a real time-saver.

Freeze homemade ice-cream in an open metal tray, whiz it in the food processor when nearly hard and then refreeze it in a box. If you are very fussy, you could repeat the process. Either way, ice-cream makers are redundant.

Sandwiches freeze. If you are making some, make a lot and have them ready for packed lunches, etc. This is also a good way to use up a roast joint.

Homemade ice lollies are much cheaper than the bought variety. Remember that freezing deadens taste so that the flavour will need to be strong.

Have a set menu for family fast day. This can become a family tradition. We always have 'eggy bread' (also known as French toast) which is bread dipped into egg beaten with milk, and fried. Children love it.

Feast day treats can also become set family traditions. Try a *Galette des Bois* at Epiphany (we have a meringue and cream version which goes down better than puff pastry), unembellished lamb, bread and salads for Maundy Thursday, sweet breads and simnel cake for Easter. Children will take pride in helping with their preparation.

Ice-cream birthday cakes are popular with children and are very quick to do. They also have to be eaten on the spot, doing away with those sticky napkin parcels! Buy any block ice-cream and shape into e.g. a castle which can then be gaily decorated. Possibly not a good idea on a hot summer's day!

Once a week, check your fridge and make a leftover meal. Cut up every leftover in little pieces and drown them in a good, creamy sauce. An easy sauce consists of melted soft cheese, with or without herbs (cheap supermarket ones). Alternatively, empty all your leftovers into the food processor with a raw onion, some flavourings and possibly an egg, shape into balls, roll in breadcrumbs and fry.

Washing-up

When I was engaged in the laundry, the Sister opposite to me, who was washing handkerchiefs, kept splashing me continually with dirty water. My first impulse was to draw back and wipe my face in order to show her that I wanted her to be more careful. The next moment, however, I saw the folly of refusing treasures thus generously offered, and I carefully refrained from betraying any annoyance. On the contrary I made such efforts to welcome the shower of dirty water that at the end of half an hour I had taken quite a fancy to the novel kind of aspersion, and resolved to return as often as possible to the place where such precious treasures were freely bestowed.

(St Thérèse of Lisieux, *Autobiography of a Saint*)

'Look, Mummy, Eleanor is helping me with the washing up!' She was, too. Brushes, soap suds, dishes, they were everywhere as Edward, aged three and a half, and Eleanor, eighteen months, stood united on a stool. I decided I needed a dishwasher, a thought I directed to Our Lady. A short time later a friend provided me with one, for which I continually bless

her. Another friend, more gallant than I, chooses not to use hers on Sundays so that she and her family can enjoy society around the sink.

You do not need to have a dishwasher to make good use of dishwasher powder. Shake a little with water into a dirty saucepan, boil for a few minutes, and burnt remains will lift off the bottom. Use a scraper and the saucepan will soon shine. Pyrex dishes can be treated in a similar way if put into a warm oven.

The best scraper is a small handheld plastic one designed for cleaning pots (mine came from a smart kitchen shop for a cheap price and is one of my most treasured possessions).

Baking tins have a tendency to rust if at all damp. Dry them in a warm oven.

Add a dash of vinegar to the rinsing water when washing glasses. A slice of lemon also makes things sparkle.

Polish as you dry the silver by making your own silver drying cloth. Mix 2 teaspoons each of Goddard's plate powder and cloudy ammonia with 2 teacups of water. Dip a small towel into the mixture until it is absorbed and hang up, retaining as much liquid as possible. Allow to drip dry. It is worth making a few towels at once, keeping spares in the drawer.

Silver spoons and forks can be boiled periodically on the stove in a large pan of plain water. Dry while still hot, and polish with a leather or soft cloth.

To clean delicate glass containers – such as vacuum flasks, glass coffee jugs, decanters – fill with warm water and add a very small amount of dishwasher powder. Leave to soak for a couple of hours. Rinse well with clean water.

Stained mugs can be similarly soaked clean using Biotex. Perhaps the dishwasher powder works too!

Before storing a Thermos, place two sugar lumps inside it to keep it from smelling musty.

First aid

Pray, hope, and don't worry.

(St Pio da Pietrelcina)

How often I have relied on their guardian angels to keep my small children from harm. Letting them learn through ordinary rough and tumble with its bruises is no bad thing. A doctor I know has commented that, while in our cottonwool society injuries to small children have gone down, accidents to the over twelves have soared because they have developed no common sense. When serious illness or other family misfortune strikes I repeat Padre Pio's wise words. If only the energy we put into worrying could be diverted into praying and hoping!

Never leave the house on an expedition with the children (especially by bicycle) without a first-aid kit. It saves many a day! A basic kit might include travel pills, paracetamol tablets, arnica pills and cream, antiseptic cream, insect repellant, cream for insect bites, burn cream, a small container of water and cotton wool for cleaning cuts, a strip of plaster and scissors, tissues, and a nappy sack in case a child is sick. Don't forget to include some sweets to boost a flagging child or take away nasty tastes.

Witch-hazel is a cure for most of the bruises, sprains and bites which need a mother's attention.

Bathing wasp stings in vinegar soothes them quickly. (A bride on her wedding day swallowed a wasp which stung her in the throat. She began to suffocate very quickly and was only saved by my mother's quick reflex in pouring vinegar down her throat!)

If you have a cold, try a small finely chopped clove of garlic mixed with a teaspoon of honey.

Arnica cream does wonders for bumps and bruises. By helping the blood to circulate, it prevents the puffing of the traumatised area. Arnica pills also help one recover from shocks (falls, operations and even giving birth).

If children object to having their hair washed, create a hood by cutting up a plastic bag in the shape of a head scarf to keep the hair away from their faces. Have to hand a dry flannel to hold against their eyes if things go wrong.

Household tricks and repairs

Blessed be the God and father of our Lord Jesus Christ, the merciful Father, the God who gives all encouragement. He it is who comforts us in all our trials; and it is this encouragement we ourselves receive from God which enables us to comfort others, whenever they have trials of their own.

(2 Corinthians 1:3-4)

At one moment we think our trials could not worsen, and at another we are overwhelmed by other people's greater tragedies and feel that we cannot bother God with our own small needs. In fact, as St Paul says, if we continue to rely daily upon God to help us in every trial, we will be in a position to help other people, just as we rely on each other for practical assistance round the house.

Keep a set of tools nearby (hammer, nails, screwdriver, strong glue…). Husbands then have reduced excuses not to go through their five minutes of home repairs when they come home. If you have no success in that quarter, make sure you have everything to hand when able friends or family come to visit.

When needing to stop for a short while during decorating, put emulsion, brushes, rollers and trays in a bin liner and tie the end. The paint will remain fresh.

If leftover paint has gone lumpy, stretch an old pair of tights over a clean tin and pour the paint slowly through.

To catch the drips when painting a ceiling, push the brush handle through a paper plate. There will be no more paint running down your wrist.

Avoid painting the glass as well as the window frame by sticking masking tape round the panes – but don't forget also to remove it quickly or it will be there for longer than you intend.

The smell of paint is neutralised by leaving out slices of onion.

Longlife light bulbs are economical and time-saving (provided they are not within range of children's missiles). Look for those with a warm light as some can be cold and rather blue.

Preparing children's parties is quicker if you self-knot balloons and then tie with ribbon or string in a loop knot. The ribbons from a bunch of balloons can be gathered together and secured on to a nail, etc., in one large joint loop knot. Releasing them later is easy.

Create a tidy edge when knitting by slipping the first and knitting the last stitches of each row.

Plants

You see, Mother, that I am but a *very little* soul, who can offer to God only *very little* things. It still happens that I frequently miss the opportunity of welcoming these small sacrifices which bring so much peace; but I am not discouraged – I bear the loss of a little peace and I try to be more watchful in the future.

(St Thérèse of Lisieux, *Autobiography of a Saint*)

If peace of soul depends upon responding rightly when things go wrong, the gardener has every opportunity to practise. Sometimes it is possible to take pre-emptive action.

Digging moles can be deterred by leaving rags soaked in petrol in their runs. Then use the earth they have crumbled for you to pot your plants.

Bury citrus peel round plants as a cat deterrent.

Put prickly holly leaves around pot plants on the patio to keep slugs away.

To save overfilling a flower vase, hold your finger just inside the rim before starting to pour. You will sense the water level even if you cannot see it clearly.

Prick cut tulips a centimetre below their heads to keep them upright. The life of poppies is preserved by burning the ends of their stalks.

Have a fixed day (or two) in the week to water house plants. Silk flowers are a very pretty alternative for forgetful gardeners.

Learning
when to stop

Come to me, all you that labour and are burdened; I will give you rest. Take my yoke upon yourselves, and learn from me; I am gentle and humble of heart; and you shall find rest for your souls. For my yoke is easy, and my burden is light.

(Matthew 11:28-30)

It is easy to bemoan the workaholics of the office and work just as relentlessly in the home. The mother of young children will inevitably be more or less continuously busy, but where possible work hard and then stop. You will be doing everybody else as well as yourself a favour.

I have yet to learn this trick myself. When with so many others I fall exhausted into bed I think with hope of my final destination and dream of all that eternal rest.

Bibliography

The Forge, by St Josemaría Escrivá, published in Spanish under the title *Forja* (1988), translated and published in English by Scepter, London (1988).

A Year with Mary, by John Paul II (1985), published in English by Catholic Book Publishing Co., New York (1986).

The Way, by St Josemaría Escrivá, published in Spanish under the title *Camino* (1939), translated and published in English in paperback by Scepter Press, Princeton (1992).

Work, by Stefan, Cardinal Wyszynski, published in Polish under the title *Duch Pracy Ludzkiej*, translated by J. Ardle McArdle and published in English by Scepter Publishers, Dublin, and Scepter Press, Chicago (1960).

Psalm 51 translated from the Hebrew by The Grail, and published in English by Collins in Fontana Books, London (1963).

The Screwtape Letters, by C.S. Lewis, published by Geoffrey Bles, The Centenary Press, London (1942).

The Way of Perfection, by St Teresa of Avila, taken

from the Spanish text edited by P. Silverio de Santa Teresa ODC and published at Burgos in 1914, translated by a Discalced Carmelite and published in English by Joseph Leighton, Edinburgh (1942).

Divine Mercy in My Soul, by St Faustina Kowalska, first published in Krakow in 1979, published in English by Marian Press, Massachusetts (1987).

Autobiography of a Saint, by St Thérèse of Lisieux, published in French under the title *L'Histoire d'une âme*, translated by Ronald Knox and published in English by The Harvill Press, London (1958).

St Paul's Second Letter to the Corinthians and the Gospel of St Matthew, taken from the Knox Bible, published by Burns Oates and Washbourne, London (1945).